AMELIA EARHART
COURAGE IN THE SKY

About the WOMEN OF OUR TIME® Series

Today more than ever, children need role models whose lives can give them the inspiration and guidance to cope with a changing world. *WOMEN OF OUR TIME*, a series of biographies focusing on the lives of twentieth-century women, is the first such series designed specifically for the 7–11 age group. International in scope, these biographies cover a wide range of personalities—from historical figures to today's headliners—in such diverse fields as politics, the arts and sciences, athletics, and entertainment. Outstanding authors and illustrators present their subjects in a vividly anecdotal style, emphasizing the childhood and youth of each woman. More than a history lesson, the *WOMEN OF OUR TIME* books offer carefully documented life stories that will inform, entertain, and inspire the young people of our time.

AMELIA EARHART

COURAGE IN THE SKY

BY MONA KERBY
Illustrated by Eileen McKeating

PUFFIN BOOKS

For Mother and Daddy with love

PUFFIN BOOKS
Published by the Penguin Group
Penguin Books USA Inc., 375 Hudson Street, New York, New York 10014, U.S.A.
Penguin Books Ltd, 27 Wrights Lane, London W8 5TZ, England
Penguin Books Australia Ltd, Ringwood, Victoria, Australia
Penguin Books Canada Ltd, 10 Alcorn Avenue, Toronto, Ontario, Canada M4V 3B2
Penguin Books (N.Z.) Ltd, 182–190 Wairau Road, Auckland 10, New Zealand

Penguin Books Ltd, Registered Offices: Harmondsworth, Middlesex, England

First published in the United States of America by Viking Penguin,
a division of Penguin Books USA Inc., 1990
Published in Puffin Books, 1992

3 5 7 9 10 8 6 4

Text copyright © Mona Kerby, 1990
Illustrations copyright © Eileen McKeating, 1990
All rights reserved

WOMEN OF OUR TIME® is a registered trademark of Viking Penguin,
a division of Penguin Books USA Inc.

LIBRARY OF CONGRESS CATALOGING-IN-PUBLICATION DATA
Kerby, Mona.
Amelia Earhart: courage in the sky / by Mona Kerby; illustrated
by Eileen McKeating.   p. cm.—(Women of our time)
Originally published: New York: Viking, 1990. (Women of our time).
Summary: Follows the life of the pilot who was the first woman to
cross the Atlantic by herself in a plane.
ISBN 0-14-034263-X
1. Earhart, Amelia, 1897–1937—Juvenile literature.   2. Air
pilots—United States—Biography—Juvenile literature.
[1. Earhart, Amelia, 1897–1937.   2. Air pilots.]   I. McKeating,
Eileen, ill.   II. Title.   III. Series: Women of our time (Puffin Books)
[TL540.E3K47 1992]   629.13'092—dc20   [B]   92-19520

Printed in the United States of America
Set in Garamond #3

CONTENTS

AMELIA EARHART
COURAGE IN THE SKY

1

"It's Just Like Flying!"

The two children stood on the roof of the toolshed and looked down at the slanting track. It stretched eight feet down to the ground. For days they had hammered. At last it was ready. With some help from their uncle, seven-year-old Millie (Amelia) and her five-year-old sister Pidge (Muriel) had built their very own "rolly" coaster.

Millie climbed into the packing crate. She folded her knees into her chest. "Let me go!" she yelled.

The box shot down the wobbly track. Within seconds, the ride was over. The girl and the crate crashed at the bottom.

Millie jumped up. She ignored her torn dress and her hurt lip. She was too excited. "Oh, Pidge," she said. "It's just like flying!"

Their parents made them tear down the roller coaster. After all, it was dangerous. But maybe Millie remembered the fun of her short "flight." When she grew up, Amelia Earhart became one of the most famous airplane pilots in the world.

Of course, on July 24, 1897, the night Amelia was born, her family wasn't thinking about airplanes or pilots. In 1897, people didn't fly. There weren't any airplanes. And even if there were, everyone knew that a woman couldn't fly one. That would have been a man's job. In those days, a woman wasn't supposed to have a career. Her place was in the home.

Amelia Mary Earhart was born in Atchison, Kansas, at the home of her grandparents, Judge Alfred Otis and his wife, Amelia. The little girl was named after both of her grandmothers. She was nicknamed Millie by her family.

Amelia's mother, Amy Otis Earhart, wrote later that Amelia was "a real watercolor baby with the bluest of blue eyes, rosy cheeks, and red lips."

Soon, Amy Earhart and baby Amelia returned to their own home in Kansas City, Kansas. Amelia's father, Edwin Stanton Earhart, worked there as a lawyer for the railroad.

Two years later, in 1899, Amelia's sister, Grace Muriel Earhart, was born. Amelia loved books, animals, and the outdoors. She could read by the time she was four. She kept a book called *Insect Life,* to identify the insects she found. Amelia's favorite books were *Peter Rabbit, Black Beauty,* and all kinds of adventure stories. Almost always, the heroes in those adventures were boys. The girl characters never did anything exciting. Amelia didn't think this was fair.

Back then, most parents thought girls should play, dress, and act differently from boys. But Amelia's parents weren't like that. Amelia loved the outdoors, so Mr. Earhart taught her to fish and play ball. And sometimes, just like a boy, Amelia jumped over fences.

It's not easy to jump fences in lacy petticoats and stockings. Mrs. Earhart had bloomers made for her daughters. The bloomers were made out of dark blue flannel, with long sleeves, high collars, and divided skirts that reached to the knees. The two girls still had to wear dark stockings and high-top shoes.

Even though some people said that bloomers weren't proper for little girls, Amelia wore them. They were perfect for walking on stilts, catching toads, and jumping fences.

Amelia didn't like to play with dolls too often. But it was fun to set them in the doll carriage and tie the carriage to her big black dog, James Ferocious. Muriel shook a bone, and James Ferocious took off running. Amelia hollered and chased from behind.

Once when James Ferocious was tied to a rope in the backyard, some boys teased him. James Ferocious barked and jumped until the rope broke. The boys scrambled onto the toolshed.

The barking awoke 6-year-old Amelia from her nap. She ran outside to her dog. "James Ferocious, you naughty dog," she said, "you've tipped over your water dish again." She patted her dog and led him inside.

Mrs. Earhart praised Amelia for her bravery, but explained that she could have been hurt. "I wasn't brave," the little girl replied, "I just didn't have time to be scared."

"Never run away," Mr. Earhart often told his daughters. Amelia took her father's words to heart. Big boys and a barking dog didn't frighten her.

In the spring of 1903, when Amelia was five, Mr. Earhart took a train to Washington, D.C. In those days, most people didn't travel very far from home. There weren't any fast planes and cars. Even so, Mr. Earhart went. He had an idea that he thought would make him rich. He had invented a holder

that held the signal flags on the backs of trains.

In Washington, Mr. Earhart learned that someone had already invented such a holder. "This news is a terrible blow," he wrote to his wife.

Later that year, Mrs. Earhart found out exactly what her husband meant. A tax collector came to the Earharts' home. *There's some mistake,* Mrs. Earhart thought. Her husband had paid the taxes. But he hadn't. Mr. Earhart had spent the money for his trip to Washington, D.C.

When Grandfather Otis found out, he was very angry. He said that Edwin Earhart was not a good husband or father. What's more, Grandfather said that Edwin would never make enough money to support his family.

Still, the Judge's disapproval didn't stop Edwin from spending money the very next year. In 1904, rather than saving, Edwin spent $100. Back then, this was a lot of money. He took his family on a week-long vacation to the World's Fair in St. Louis, Missouri.

For the first time in her life, 6-year-old Amelia rode an elephant and a Ferris wheel. Because she was too little to ride the roller coaster, Amelia decided to make one in her own backyard.

Amelia learned more than how to make a roller coaster. She was learning lessons that would last her a lifetime. *If you want to do something,* her father explained, *you must be willing to pay the price.*

Because her father spent the money, Grandfather Otis disliked him. Grandfather's disapproval was the price Mr. Earhart paid so that his little girls could enjoy themselves.

Amelia watched her father's example and remembered. Years later, when she wanted to fly, she would be willing to pay the price.

2

"Sizz-boom-bah!"

Millie squatted down and held her head close to the porch for a good look. She smiled. Her racer was fat and long and slinky. The leaf and the blade of grass made a perfect carriage and harness. She glanced over at Pidge. Her sister's worm was ready, too. *"Go,"* Millie shouted, and the worm race was on.

Worm races were just one of the things Amelia dreamed up to do during the summers in Atchison, Kansas. Between 1905 and 1908, Amelia and Muriel lived much of the time with their grandparents. Their parents had moved to Des Moines, Iowa. Mr. Earhart got a good job with the railroad. When he travelled, his wife went with him. The girls remained in Atchison until their mother found a house she thought was right. Besides, Mrs. Earhart thought the schools were better there.

These times were happy. Amelia and Muriel spent hours reading the books and magazines in their grandfather's library. They also played with their cousins, Lucy and Katherine Challis, nicknamed Toot and Katch. The girls invented their own vocabulary. A house was called a "shouse." Grocery boys were called "garshee boys." Grasshoppers were called "hannibals."

On hot summer evenings, the four cousins gathered the old skins of grasshoppers. Amelia led the way, as they slowly walked to the back of their grandparents' house. Here they placed the grasshoppers' skins on a tree stump.

Kneeling, they tapped their heads on the trunk. "Kow-tou-kow-tou to the Great Ken How," they chanted.

Amelia struck a match to the dried grasshopper skins. While the skins burned, the girls marched around the tree stump singing, "Grumpa, grumpa, dance, dance, dance." At the very end, they shouted at the top of their lungs, "Hannibal! Hannibal! Sizz-boom-bah!"

On Christmas eve in 1906, the year Amelia was nine, her parents arrived loaded with gifts. Two presents were exactly what Amelia wanted—a boy's sled and a gun. Of course, Judge Otis didn't approve of such things for little girls. Perhaps this was one reason that Mr. Earhart gave them to Amelia.

With the new sled, Amelia didn't sit straight as girls were supposed to do. She did "belly flops" like the boys did. Once, as she was speeding down a hill, she saw a cart and a horse on the road below. Amelia shouted, but the driver didn't hear. She couldn't stop and she couldn't turn. There was only one thing to do. Amelia slid between the horse's legs.

Amelia wanted the .22 rifle to shoot the rats in the barn. One evening, she shot a rat but it didn't die. Amelia waited nearly an hour before she saw the rat again. This time she shot and killed it. She was late for dinner, breaking one of Grandmother's rules. Amelia accepted her punishment—the gun was taken away.

This was probably a good idea. The barn was shot full of holes. The man who worked for Amelia's grandparents said, "Amelia gets an idea and, by gosh, she stays right with it. Dinner or no dinner, punishment or not, she wanted to get the rats."

As a little girl and as a grown woman, Amelia was often asked why she wanted to do something. She

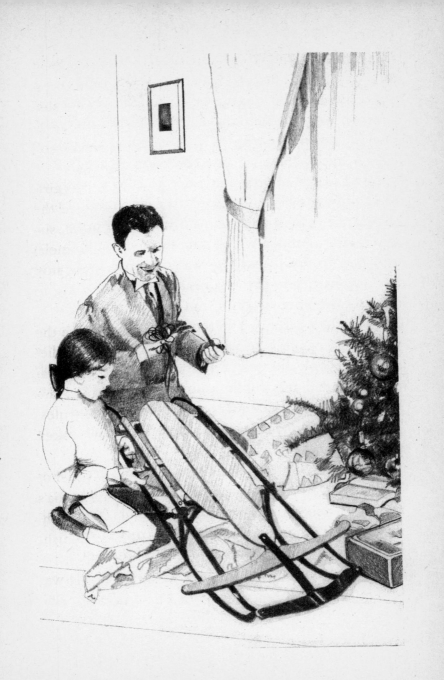

always replied simply and stubbornly, "Because I want to."

For her tenth birthday in 1907, Amelia saw her first airplane at the Iowa State Fair in Des Moines. She thought it was ugly with its rusty wire and wood. The plane, called a biplane, had two pairs of wings. The pilot sat in the middle and wore goggles so that the wind and bugs wouldn't get in his eyes. Another man started the plane by turning a big wooden propeller. Years later, Amelia wrote that she didn't pay much attention to the plane. She was too busy looking at her new hat made out of a peach basket.

In the summer of 1908, the Earhart girls went to live with their parents. Their new home in Des Moines was a big change for the sisters. They didn't have a maid or a cook. Instead of attending a private school, they attended the public school. By the next year, however, Mr. Earhart was promoted to a better job. The Earhart family moved to a larger house and hired servants.

As a family, they attended concerts and art shows. They belonged to a magazine club, sharing magazines with their neighbors. During the summers, they took vacations in Minnesota. They took trips in their father's private railroad car. The car had a small living room, bedroom, and kitchen. Everything seemed wonderful.

But it wasn't. Mr. Earhart began to drink too much alcohol. Several times a week he shuffled home from work. His speech was sloppy and thick. Even though he went to a hospital for treatment, he couldn't seem to stop drinking too much.

Amelia, Muriel, and Mrs. Earhart didn't let the neighbors see their sadness. They pretended everything was fine. Still, the Judge and Grandmother Otis knew that something was wrong.

In February, 1912, Grandmother Otis died. In her will, she left her money to her four children. The will stated, however, that Amy's share was to be held by the bank for twenty years or until Edwin Earhart died. Mr. Earhart was ashamed and embarrassed. He began to drink even more.

And finally, in 1913, he lost his job. Amelia was sixteen years old. She had to leave her high school and her friends. The Earhart family left for St. Paul, Minnesota, where her father found work as a clerk in a railroad office.

Since Amelia and Muriel were new, they weren't invited to many parties. They didn't have the money to join the fancy skating and social clubs. In December of that year, they looked forward to a party at their church. Back then, fathers brought their daughters to dances. Mr. Earhart promised to come home in plenty of time. Instead, he came home late. He was drunk.

Muriel cried, but Amelia refuse to shed a tear. She threw out the marshmallows which they had planned to have with their hot chocolate after the dance. She tore up the Christmas decorations.

Since there wasn't money for spring clothes, Amelia took matters into her own hands. She found curtain material in the attic and made skirts for herself and for Muriel. They dyed their skirts and painted their old hats and wore them on Easter morning.

Amelia didn't complain. In fact, she managed to make Muriel laugh. If it rains, she warned, get under shelter before you leave a trail of green dye.

Things didn't get better. Mr. Earhart was offered another job. This time, they moved to Springfield, Missouri. Their family arrived in the fall of 1915 with all of their belongings. But a man who was supposed to retire had changed his mind. There was no work for Mr. Earhart after all.

Mrs. Earhart made a painful decision. She left her husband. She took the girls to Chicago and stayed with friends. Brokenhearted, Mr. Earhart lived with his sister in Kansas City. Since he couldn't get a job as a lawyer with the railroad, he opened his own law office.

In Chicago, Amelia entered Hyde Park High School. The English teacher had trouble controlling the class. Amelia didn't want to spend the entire year learning nothing. She talked the principal into letting her read in the library during English period. Although this was a way to learn, it was not a way to make friends. The words under her picture in the school yearbook read, "The girl in brown who walks alone."

It was almost as if the students had seen into the future. Amelia Earhart would achieve great fame all by herself. But first, she received some welcome help from her family.

3

The Little Red Plane

In the summer of 1916, Amy, Amelia, and Muriel rejoined Edwin Earhart in Kansas City. He was overjoyed. Edwin wanted to help his family again. For this reason, he talked Mrs. Earhart into going to court to break Grandmother Otis's will. Mrs. Earhart's brother, who took care of her money, had lost much of it on bad business deals. The court ruled in Mrs. Earhart's favor. She used the money to send her daughters to good schools.

In the fall of 1916, Amelia arrived at the Ogontz School in Rydal, Pennsylvania. She was an excellent

student and an outstanding athlete. She liked to play hockey, basketball, and tennis. Her letters to her mother were happy and filled with the details of her school activities.

Amelia was tall and slender, and the girls quickly nicknamed her Butterball. They liked her and Amelia liked them. Still, she was not afraid to speak her mind.

During her first year at school, Amelia belonged to a secret club. When she realized that some students had not been invited to join, she asked the members to include the other girls. They refused. Amelia went to the headmistress, who ran the school, and asked that another club be added for these girls. Instead, the headmistress did away with the secret clubs.

On another occasion, Amelia argued that the students should have the freedom to discuss and read anything they wanted. These actions set her apart from the other girls. But, as always, whenever Amelia believed in something, she was willing to "walk alone."

For Christmas of 1917, Amelia and her mother visited Muriel in Toronto, Canada, where Muriel was at school. One day, as Amelia walked down King Street, she saw something that changed her life. She met four young men using crutches. Each of them was missing a leg.

The young men had been hurt in battle. For three years, there had been war. The Great War, as it was called then, lasted four years. (Almost 25 years later, the Great War was renamed World War I, when World War II began.) The Great War destroyed countries, governments, homes, and lives. Nearly 10 million soldiers were killed. More than 15 million people were wounded.

While at school, Amelia had knitted socks for soldiers. Until she met the soldiers in Toronto, however, she didn't fully understand the horrors of fighting.

Right then and there, Amelia made a decision. With her mother's permission, she did not return to school. Instead, she stayed in Toronto and became a nurse's aide.

She worked from seven in the morning until seven

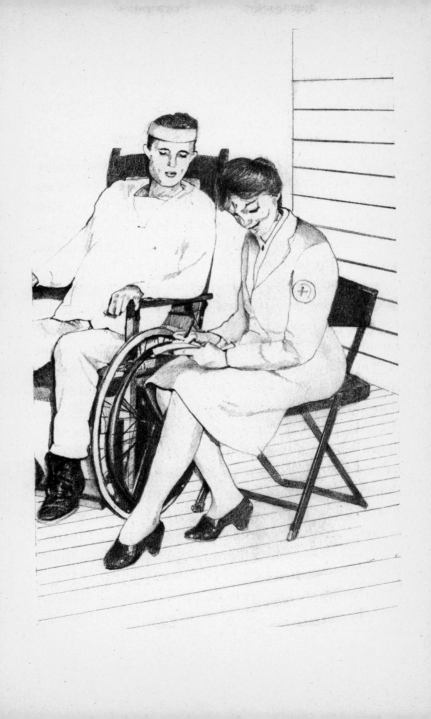

at night, with two hours off in the afternoon. At the hospital, Amelia gave medicine, scrubbed floors, prepared meals, gave back rubs, and wrote letters for soldiers.

When Amelia had spare time, she liked to ride a wild horse named Dynamite. One soldier told her that she rode Dynamite the way he flew his plane. Sometimes the ride was smooth and sometimes it was rough. Amelia stayed on the horse.

Something else caused Amelia to think about planes. One afternoon at an air show in Toronto, Amelia and a friend were watching a pilot doing stunts in the air. Perhaps to tease the girls, the pilot headed for them. Amelia's friend screamed and ran, but Amelia stood still. She heard the sound of the motor. She felt the wind on her face. She was excited. Years later, she wrote, "I believe that little red airplane said something to me as it swished by."

When the war was over in 1918, Amelia became ill with pneumonia (say, "new-MOAN-ya"). Muriel had moved to Northampton, Massachusetts. Amelia stayed with her sister and spent nearly a year resting and recovering. She bought an old banjo and learned to read music. Like her father, Amelia played by ear. Once she heard a melody, she could then play it. She also signed up for a five-week course in car repair.

In the fall of 1919, she entered Columbia University in New York City. She wanted to be a doctor. She had always liked science and she did well in her classes. For fun, Amelia took a course in French poetry. And for excitement, she used to sit on top of the Columbia library dome. Somehow, Amelia discovered where the key to the roof was kept. Dressed in her hat and long skirt, she would crawl out onto the roof. There she sat on the sloping roof, hugging her knees and staring at the buildings below her.

By the spring of 1920, Amelia decided she really

did not want to study medicine. Her parents had moved to Los Angeles, California, and they asked her to live with them. Even though her father was no longer drinking, they weren't happy. Amelia wanted to help.

The Earharts lived in a large home and rented out some of the rooms. One of the renters was a young chemical engineer by the name of Sam Chapman. Sam and Amelia spent many hours together. Sam loved Amelia. He asked her to marry him, and for years, he waited for her answer. She always said no.

Sam believed that a wife should stay at home and take care of children. But a marriage like that hadn't made Amelia's parents happy. Besides, she insisted, women should have the same freedom as men. More than anything, Amelia wanted to be independent. She wanted a career of her own.

Still, a career in flying was the farthest thing from Amelia's mind. In World War I, a few thousand pilots took part in the bombing and fighting. But in 1920, stunt flying was about the only thing to do with a plane. For whatever reason, Amelia began attending air shows. Perhaps she remembered the little red plane.

One day, Amelia and her father stood on the sidelines and watched. "Dad, please ask that officer how long it takes to fly," she said.

Mr. Earhart did. He told his daughter it took five to ten hours to learn.

"Please find out how much lessons cost," Amelia continued.

"The answer to that is a thousand dollars. But why do you want to know?"

Amelia wasn't really sure. A few days later, one of the pilots took her up in his plane. From her seat behind the pilot, Amelia saw the ocean. She saw the Hollywood Hills. And suddenly, everything became clear to Amelia. There was only one thing to do. As she wrote later in her book, *The Fun of It,* "I knew I myself had to fly."

4

Top Speed

Amelia turned over in bed and crackled. With each toss and turn, she crackled some more. The next morning, she looked at herself in the mirror. It was better. Still, she slept in it another night.

It was 1922 and Amelia had just bought a real leather jacket. Now, she looked like a true flyer. But the other pilots' jackets were worn. Hers was too shiny and new. So, for three nights, Amelia slept in her coat. "There just had to be some wrinkles," she explained.

Soon after her first plane ride, Amelia signed up

for lessons. She expected her parents to pay for them. They didn't. Mr. and Mrs. Earhart didn't mind if Amelia wanted to fly. But they didn't have a thousand dollars to spare.

Amelia didn't give up. She took a job in the post office. To earn some extra money, she did some photography work. She also found a flyer who would teach her and let her pay when she had the money. Her teacher's name was Neta Snook and she was one of the first women pilots in the world. Like Amelia, she wore a leather jacket, wrinkled.

When Amelia flew, she also wore a padded leather helmet, goggles, shirt, scarf, tight-fitting pants, and leather boots that laced up to her knees. One reason she dressed this way was because she wanted to look exactly like the other pilots, or aviators, as they were called. ("AY-vee-ay-ters.") A woman pilot was called an aviatrix ("ay-vee-AY-tricks"). But the main reason she dressed this way was because flying was dirty, dusty, and rough.

In those days, runways weren't concrete; they were dirt or grass. At every takeoff and landing, there was a whirlwind of dust. Up in the air in open cockpits, aviators felt the snow, sleet, rain, and hail. In cold weather, they smeared grease on their faces to keep them from freezing. Leather coats and helmets protected aviators from the weather and from bumps and scrapes during rough rides. Goggles kept bugs and dirt out of their eyes.

At first, airplanes were known by their British name, "aeroplanes" ("AIR-uh-playns"). They were also called ships. In a way, they sailed in the air just as boats sailed in the sea.

These aeroplanes were very light. On the ground, aviators pushed them around by their tails. Planes didn't have a metal body. Instead, they were covered with cloth. In the air, top speed was 80 miles per hour. This is not much faster than the speed limit on today's highways.

Aviators steered their "ships" with their hands on a control stick and with their feet on a rudder bar. They made the aeroplanes go up and down by moving the control stick forward and backward. They turned their planes from left to right by moving the control stick from side to side.

They also turned the plane by pressing on the rudder bar with their feet. This bar was attached to the rudder, a wooden flap on the tail of the plane. In the air, the rudder bar shook and shivered and throbbed. In fact, it vibrated so much that after a few minutes, Amelia's feet always went to sleep.

She loved every minute of it. "It's so breathtakingly beautiful up there," she explained. "I want to fly whenever I can." Soon, other aviators were calling Amelia a natural. Not only could she fly, but she could also repair a plane's engine and sew up the rips in the plane's body.

But in those days, women were not supposed to fly. Plenty of people, including Sam, reminded Amelia that women should be ladies. They should pin their hair neatly in a bun, get married, and stay home.

No doubt, Amelia worried about the proper way to act. In the end, however, she made up her own mind. In the summer of 1922, she cut off her long hair. Then she bought a bright yellow secondhand Kinner Canary Aeroplane. She spent all of her savings and all of Muriel's savings. She even used her mother's money to buy the plane.

And, she earned the only kind of flying license issued at the time. There were possibly twelve women in the entire world with such a license. Amelia Earhart was one of them.

That fall, Amelia set her first air record by becoming the first woman to fly at 14,000 feet. A few weeks later, she was trying to fly higher, when trouble hit. Blinded by snow and clouds, Amelia had no idea if she was flying right side up, sideways, or upside down. She spun the plane nose down, turning over and over for 12,000 feet. At 3,000 feet, the clouds broke and

Amelia could see. When she landed, she was shaking. As she told her friends, good pilots don't worry too much.

For the next few years, Amelia worked during the week and flew on the weekends. After all, there weren't any careers for women in flying. She was flying for the sheer "fun of it." Then, once again, something happened that changed her life.

In 1924, Amelia's parents divorced. They were no longer happy together. Edwin remained in California. Amy wanted to go East to Boston, where Muriel was in school. Amelia sold her plane and bought a bright yellow roadster, a type of car with a cloth top. In the 1920s, there weren't any paved highways, just dirt roads. There weren't many gasoline stations and no fast-food restaurants along the way.

Late in the spring of 1925, Amelia and her mother headed East in Amelia's car. They set out to cross the entire country, alone. This trip might have stopped some people. It didn't stop Amelia.

5

The Important Question

Amelia and her mother rolled into Boston. Their car windows were full of stickers from all the places they had visited.

Within a week, Amelia was in the hospital. For years, she had suffered from terrible headaches. Flying had made them worse. In the Boston hospital, a piece of bone was removed from Amelia's nose. This operation helped her sinuses to drain and made her head feel better. Unfortunately, however, any time Amelia was under stress, she got a headache.

But a little pain never stopped Amelia for long. Soon, she was ready for work. She found a job helping families who were new to the United States. She taught the children English and other useful skills. Since many of them had never ridden in a car, Amelia often drove the children around the block.

People liked Amelia. She was quiet and pleasant. But in 1927, Amelia Earhart was an unusual woman. Though few people at work knew it, Amelia was spending her spare time with planes. She flew them, repaired them, and talked about them with other pilots. Some of her family thought she was odd. Only her mother encouraged her. Years later, Amy wrote, "I realized that if she wanted to be a flyer someone in the family had to be interested."

Certainly Sam Chapman didn't understand Amelia. He changed jobs and followed her to Boston. To Sam's way of thinking, it was time for Amelia to become his wife and stop these foolish ideas of having a career. After all, she was thirty years old. Amelia told her sister, "I know what I want to do and I expect to do it, married or single."

But more than likely, Amelia had no idea what she wanted to do. One afternoon in 1928, when she was teaching, she received a phone call. "Tell 'em I'm busy," Amelia said.

"Says it's important," came the reply.

When Amelia picked up the phone, a man asked her a question which changed her life.

She agreed to meet with the man and some of his friends that evening. Their talk centered on the important question, "Would you like to fly the Atlantic?" There was only one answer for Amelia. "Yes," she replied.

In 1928, only seven planes had successfully crossed the Atlantic Ocean. No woman had ever made the trip.

Mrs. Amy Guest of England bought a plane and hired a crew. She wanted to be the first woman to fly across the Atlantic Ocean. Her family was afraid for her to make the trip. She asked George Palmer Putnam of the American publishing company to find a woman pilot to take her place.

The year before, Putnam's company had published the pilot Charles Lindbergh's story, *We*, about his own

flight across the ocean. Putnam was eager to sell another book and make some more money. He found a woman pilot—Amelia Earhart.

Mrs. Guest paid for the flight. She made Amelia captain of the plane, and said that Amelia would make all the decisions during the flight. However, Amelia would not fly the plane since she did not have as much experience as the crew. And she would not get any money. The pilot Wilmer (Bill) Stulz received $20,000 while the mechanic Lou (Slim) Gordon received $5,000.

Amelia agreed to Mrs. Guest's rules. Amelia knew that this flight would open doors for her later, both in writing and in flying. Besides, Amelia explained, she wanted to do it for the fun of it.

For its time, the plane, named the *Friendship,* was gigantic. With huge tanks of gas, the 3-engine plane weighed more than 5 tons. In some places, the wings were 26 inches thick, with a total wing span of 72 feet. (The wings were about as long as 5 of today's midsize cars.) So that it could land on water, the landing wheels were replaced with huge boat-shaped parts called pontoons. And just in case the plane went down, it was painted bright orange, making it easy to spot.

The crew did their work in secret. They didn't want another woman pilot to hear of their plans and beat them. And if their flight failed, they didn't want the whole world to know about it.

Not even Amelia's family knew about the planned flight. In case she died, Amelia wrote a will and left letters for her parents. To her father she wrote, "Hooray for the last grand adventure! I wish I had won, but it was worthwhile anyway." She wrote her mother, "My life has really been very happy and I don't mind contemplating its end in the midst of it."

Finally, after months of work, everything was ready. Amelia carried a toothbrush, a comb, a handkerchief, and a tube of cold cream. She didn't even bring a change of underwear. She wore her old favorite flying clothes, including her leather jacket. She borrowed a heavy fur-lined jumpsuit.

On the morning of June 4, 1928, Amelia and her crew huddled in the *Friendship*. The engines roared to full power, but the plane refused to fly. They pitched out 6 of the 5-gallon cans of gasoline, leaving themselves only 2 cans. Again they tried. No luck. Another pilot, Louis Gower, had hoped to go with them. Without a word, he got his bag and jumped off the plane.

For the third time that morning, the engines roared. The plane struggled. Then slowly but surely, it flew. They were off. Headlines splashed across the Boston newspapers: *Girl Pilot Dares the Atlantic.* The secret was out. The world was watching Amelia.

Their plan was to stop briefly at Trepassey, Newfoundland, for more fuel. When they arrived, the weather was terrible. Fog covered the island. A cold Arctic wind blew in. The *Friendship* was trapped.

They stayed two weeks. For fun, Amelia and Slim played cards. The pilot got drunk. G.P. Putnam sent a telegram to Amelia: "Suggest you turn in and have your laundering done." Amelia replied: "Thanks fatherly telegram. No washing necessary. Socks underwear worn out. Shirt lost to Slim at Rummy. Cheerio. AE."

At last the weather changed. By 6:30 on the morning of June 17, Amelia and her crew were in the plane, ready to leave. The waters were rough. Once again, the plane refused to fly. To make it lighter, they threw out everything they could spare—the movie camera, a thermos of cocoa for Amelia, extra gas, life jackets. Three times they tried. At 11:40 A.M., the plane shook violently and rose from the sea. They were in the air.

37

The *Friendship* headed east toward the British Isles. Fog, snowstorms, rainstorms, and thick rolling clouds met them head on. Each time rain hit the engines, they sputtered and coughed. Bill did most of the flying. Amelia never flew. Instead, she remained in the back, kneeling beisde a window and keeping notes on their flight.

At 8 o'clock that evening, the *Friendship* lost all radio contact. Bill held the plane on course by watching the control panel and by looking at the stars. It was freezing cold. The engines roared in their ears. The black of night surrounded them. They were all alone.

Day dawned and still the *Friendship* flew. And then an engine stalled. The gas tanks were almost empty. At 8:50 A.M., Bill nosed the plane down to get a better look.

A ship! Where were they?

Bill tried the radio. It didn't work. Slim wrote a note, which Amelia tied to an orange. Leaning out the cargo door, she tried to bomb the boat with the orange. It plopped in the sea. Should they land beside the ship or should they continue on their course?

The *Friendship* flew on. Slim bit into a sandwich.

And then he saw something. He pointed it out to Bill. What happened next is best described by Amelia. "I think Sam yelled. I know the sandwich went flying out the window. It was land!"

6

Tomato Juice and a 20-Dollar Bill

It was an unusual welcome. Bill, Slim, and Amelia sat on the plane and waited. No one came. For a straight 20 hours and 40 minutes, they had flown 2,000 miles over the Atlantic Ocean. In all that time, Amelia had eaten 3 oranges and a handful of malted-milk candy balls. None of them had slept much. Now they sat on the plane while it rocked gently in the water. Rain pattered on the metal roof. Amelia yelled and waved at the fishermen. The fishermen waved back and went on with their work.

The silence did not last long. In a few hours, they

went ashore and learned that they had landed at Burry Port, Wales. The next morning, they flew on to Southampton, England. Here they met Mrs. Guest, the woman who had made their trip possible. And suddenly, everyone wanted to meet Amelia.

Telegrams, messages, gifts, and invitations arrived from all over the world. U.S. president Calvin Coolidge praised Amelia's courage. The British government asked Amelia to speak. The Prince of Wales asked her to dance. Back home, 32 cities asked her to visit.

Newspapers called her "Lady Lindy." She looked like Charles Lindbergh, they reported. Just like him, with her quiet, modest, and sincere way, Amelia captured the hearts of the people. She tried to explain that she hadn't done anything special. She praised the skills of Bill Stulz, the pilot. She had just gone along for the ride, she added.

Amelia felt she didn't deserve this attention. She made a decision. "The next time I fly anywhere," she said, "I shall do it alone."

Amelia stayed ten days in England and sailed home. In a New York City parade, people lined the streets, throwing confetti and cheering for Amelia. From the very beginning, G.P. Putnam managed everything. Amelia was grateful for his help. The *Friendship* crew visited New York, Chicago, and Medford, Massachusetts, Amelia's hometown at the time. After that, Amelia stayed at G.P.'s mansion and wrote her first book, *20 Hours and 40 Minutes.*

As soon as she finished, Amelia was off again. She decided to fly across the country, making stops along the way. Since there weren't many airports, Amelia landed along highways, and in fields. Once in Pecos, Texas, she landed right in the middle of Main Street. When she returned to New York, Amelia learned that she had set a record. She became the first woman to make a solo (by herself) round-trip flight across the United States.

G.P. set up speaking engagements for Amelia all over the country. She flew alone, speaking in the morning and flying to the next town in the afternoon. Rather than wear her leather jacket and helmet, Amelia dressed in skirts and hats. By looking like a "lady," Amelia wanted to show that flying wasn't just for men. Someday, she said, "Women will be free to live their lives as men are free."

Amelia made those words come true for herself. In the next few years, she continued to achieve. In August, 1929, she finished third in the first Women's Air Derby, a race from California to Ohio. She and 98 women pilots formed a club called "The Ninety-Nines." As an editor for the magazine *Cosmopolitan,* Amelia wrote articles on topics such as safety in flying, letting a daughter fly, and pilot training. On July 6, 1930, Amelia set a speed record by flying 181 m.p.h. She even flew an autogiro, one of the first helicopters, across the country. And Amelia wrote her second book, *The Fun of It*.

Still, these achievements were simple compared to what she did on February 7, 1931. On that day, 33-year-old Amelia did something that truly scared her. She married.

G.P. Putnam proposed 6 times. The last time, both of them were standing beside her plane. He asked; she patted his arm, nodded, and then crawled in her plane and took off.

On her wedding day, Amelia wore an old brown suit. She gave G.P. a letter, asking him to "let me go in a year if we find no happiness together." Amelia insisted on keeping her last name. They didn't take a honeymoon.

Without a word, G.P. accepted Amelia's strange behavior. This must have been hard, because he was not a quiet, easygoing man. Twelve years older than Amelia, G.P. had already been married two times. He was attractive, talkative, and bossy. As one of the owners of a worldwide publishing company, G.P. was used to getting his way. He had money and power.

But he was not famous. Perhaps this is one reason G.P. was attracted to Amelia. She was known all over

the world. Amelia's fame made life exciting for G.P.

Sometimes G.P. made people mad. Reporters never liked to interview Amelia when he was around because he did the talking. And it seemed as if G.P. was always cooking up business deals to make some money from Amelia's name. Amelia Earhart luggage and Amelia Earhart sports clothes became popular items.

Amelia never did ask G.P. to "let her go." She travelled constantly and wasn't home much. She even took a job at Purdue University in West Lafayette, Indiana. She helped girls in finding jobs, or careers.

It's not enough to be someone's wife, she told them.

While their marriage might have seemed odd for the times, it worked for G.P. and Amelia. He gave Amelia freedom. What's more, whenever she wanted to do something, G.P. helped her all the way.

At breakfast one morning in the spring of 1932, Amelia happened to say that she would like to fly the Atlantic Ocean solo. By noon, G.P. had made the arrangements. Amelia met with experts in flying and weather forecasting. G.P. took care of publicity and raising money.

Within a month, everything was ready. Amelia left from an airport in New Jersey, heading north for Newfoundland. Just as she did for her first trip across the Atlantic, Amelia chose the shortest route over the ocean.

She left Newfoundland on May 20 at 7:12 in the evening, exactly 5 years after Lindbergh made his famous flight. She carried two cans of tomato juice, a comb, a toothbrush, and a 20-dollar bill. At 11:00 P.M., she hit a storm. The next 10 hours were tough.

She could not see anything out of the cockpit. She had to trust the plane's instruments. Then the altimeter broke, which measured how high the plane flew. A reserve tank of gas began to leak. Sparks of flame burst from an exhaust pipe. The entire plane shook. Ice formed on the wings and Amelia spun the plane. She almost hit the ocean.

But she made it. The next morning, she landed safely in Ireland.

In June, after Amelia was home, the National Geographic Society honored Amelia. They introduced her as the first woman to fly over the Atlantic, the first woman to fly it alone, and the first *person* in the world to cross it twice. She received the Society's special Gold Medal. President Herbert Hoover, Supreme Court justices, senators, and congressmen were there. They all clapped for Amelia.

With her usual modesty, Amelia replied, "My flight has added nothing to aviation. However, I hope that the flight has meant something to women in aviation."

People all over the world admired Amelia's courage. By now, she was rich and could have easily retired. Instead, she continued to test herself in the air.

In January, 1935, Amelia announced she would fly from Hawaii to California, some 2,400 miles across the Pacific Ocean. Ten men had died while attempting the crossing. So far, only one man had successfully completed the flight. Newspaper headlines announced that Amelia's proposed flight was a publicity stunt. Amelia paid no attention.

She was in the air for more than 15 hours, but this

time the flight was easy. The weather was good. Her plane had the latest equipment. One invention was a two-way radio telephone. Thousands of people tuned in to hear Amelia talk with G.P., who was still in Hawaii. While Amelia flew, she listened to the music of the Metropolitan Opera in New York City. She sipped hot chocolate under a starry sky.

When she arrived the next day in Oakland, California, nearly 10,000 people greeted her. President Franklin D. Roosevelt sent her a letter. "You've scored again," he wrote.

No one had any idea what Amelia was planning to do next.

7

"Because I Want To"

Reporters crowded around Amelia. *Why do you want to fly around the world,* they shouted at her.

Amelia grinned, then chuckled. She was 38 years old. The reporters wrote that Amelia looked like a young girl with her freckled nose, short hair, and slim build.

"Because I want to," she said simply.

In 1936, planes were becoming common. Already there were passenger planes seating 10 people and flying from coast to coast. Planes were even beginning

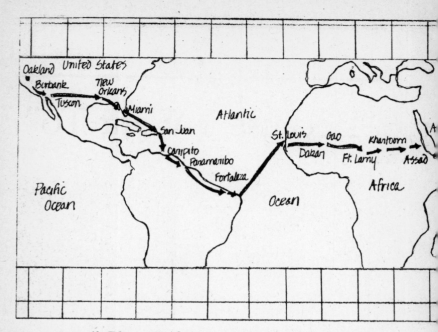

to carry mail. Planes had crossed the oceans, explored the North and South Poles, and flown around the top of the world. But no one had ever dared to make the longest and most dangerous trip of all—a trip around the middle of the earth at the equator—25,000 miles of deserts, jungles, and ocean.

Amelia stood before the news reporters. "I think I have just one more long flight in my system," she said.

The first step was getting the plane. Amelia used the money she earned from her speeches. G.P. made a deal to sell 25,000 envelopes which read, *Round* *

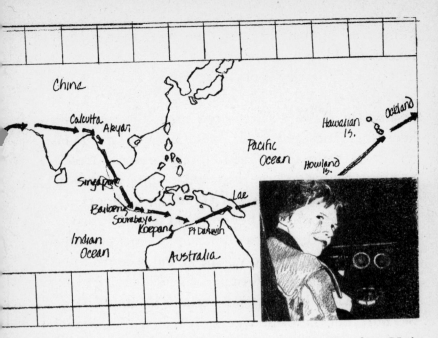

the * World * Flight * Amelia Earhart. Purdue University gave $40,000 toward the purchase of Amelia's plane.

The Lockheed *Electra* was the finest plane in the world. With a metal body, it could fly as fast as 210 m.p.h. and travel nonstop for 4,500 miles. In the cockpit, there were 100 dials and levers hooked up to the latest inventions. With a flip of a switch, the autopilot flew the plane. Just like a homing pigeon, the radio direction finder identified a radio "homing" signal and could fly the plane to that very spot. Also, there was a two-way telephone system. People called the *Electra*

49

a "flying laboratory" because there were so many new inventions for Amelia to try.

It took more than a year to get ready. On the morning of March 17, 1937, Amelia left California and headed for Hawaii. Three crew members went with her. Paul Mantz served as copilot. Captain Harry Manning worked the radio. Fred Noonan navigated, plotting their course on large maps and keeping them from getting lost. They arrived in Hawaii in 15 hours and 43 minutes. Amelia and her crew had set a new record.

On March 20, the heavily loaded *Electra* prepared for takeoff. As it picked up speed and rose from the runway, the right wing dropped. Sparks flew; the *Electra* dropped on its belly and crashed. Luckily, no one was hurt, but the plane was badly damaged. It would have to be repaired.

"Will you give up your flight now?" reporters asked.

"Of course not," Amelia replied. "I shall certainly try again."

And she did. The preparations started all over again—more money, more gasoline and supplies sent to countries where they expected to land, more test flying, more Amelia Earhart envelopes to sell. Amelia studied world maps and weather charts. This time, she would fly east rather than west. This time, there would be only one other crew member—Fred Noonan.

Fred was considered to be one of the best navigators

in the business. This was important because the plane's homing device worked only within a few hundred miles of a radio beam. It was also important because Amelia was not a good navigator.

To keep the plane on course, Fred studied the stars; he recorded the speed of the plane; he watched the time. Over land, he looked for landmarks. Over the ocean, however, there was nothing. Their lives depended on Fred's navigation. Fred had lost one job because he was an alcoholic. He promised Amelia he would not drink. She believed him.

In 1937, the Morse code was the best way of sending messages over long distances. Sent over the radio, each letter had its own signal, or beeping sound. Neither Fred nor Amelia knew the Morse code. Instead, Amelia used one of the new voice phones which did not always work. Amelia wasn't worried. She also removed a 250-foot radio antenna. This would have increased her chances of being heard. But she needed the space, she explained.

They left California on May 19, 1937. G.P. and a mechanic flew with them. This time they headed east and arrived in Miami on May 23. For a few days, Amelia worked on the plane and rested. G.P. asked Amelia to make the trip alone. He always wanted her flights to get lots of attention. Amelia said no.

And for the second time, early on the morning of

June 1, 1937, Amelia took off for her round-the-world trip. She never saw her husband again.

For 32 days, every major newspaper in the world headlined Amelia's flight. *Aviatrix Lands in Puerto Rico Safely. Amelia Hops 750 Miles to Venezuela. Amelia Makes Atlantic Hop to African Coast. Earhart Crosses Sahara Desert. Amelia on Nonstop Hop to Calcutta. Amelia at Java: To Overhaul Plane.* Sometimes, Amelia wrote the articles herself. A few times, Amelia and G.P. were able to talk by telephone. Their conversations were heard over the radio and later printed in the papers.

In the days before TV, Amelia's description of different lands and people enchanted the world. She described a bumpy camel ride. She wrote that the Red Sea was really blue. And Amelia reported that pilots in Pakistan were not allowed to wear false teeth because during rough rides they might choke on their teeth.

Amelia and Fred left Lae, New Guinea, on July 3. Two more stops and they would be home.

They faced the most difficult flight of their entire lives. They would have to spend 18 hours in the air, crossing 2,500 miles of ocean. Because the plane was so heavy, Amelia did not carry any extra fuel. Their target was tiny Howland Island—one mile long, a half-mile wide and a mere 20 feet above sea level. Fred could not make even one tiny mistake in his navigation. If he did, they would never find the island.

For hours, they flew without any radio contact. They were too far away to be heard. The ship U.S.S. *Itasca* waited off the coast near Howland Island, ready to receive and send radio signals. As Amelia neared the island, she could have used her radio direction finder and flown straight to the airstrip. But she didn't turn it on. She never knew that the ship was sending her the homing beam.

At 2:45 in the morning, the *Itasca* heard Amelia say, "Cloudy and overcast." They called Amelia. She didn't answer.

At 6:45, Amelia pleaded, "Please take a bearing on us." She wanted them to find her plane and tell her which direction to fly. She whistled into the microphone, but the sound was too weak for the men to figure out where she was.

The *Itasca* called Amelia on the radio at 7:18, 7:19, 7:25, 7:26, and 7:30. She never answered.

At 7:42, Amelia's voice was high and scared. "We must be on you," she said, "but cannot see you. But gas is running low. Been unable to reach you by radio."

The *Itasca* repeated the Morse code sound for the letter A, dot, dash, or *di dah, di dah, di dah.*

Even though Amelia could not send a message in

Morse code, she did know the code for the first letter in her name. She called out, "We are receiving your signals."

At 8:45, the *Itasca* heard Amelia again. She explained that they were flying back and forth, from north to south. "We are running north and south," she said. That was the end. No one ever heard from Amelia Earhart again.

For two weeks, the United States Navy searched for Amelia and Fred. Planes and ships crossed over 250,000 square miles of ocean and islands. The *Electra* was never found.

The disappearance of Amelia Earhart shocked the world. People could not believe she was dead. Rumors spread. She was on a spy mission for the U.S. government. She was captured by the Japanese. She

changed her name and became a housewife in New Jersey.

More than likely, Amelia drowned, but no one really knows what happened. It's still a mystery—and perhaps that's one reason the story of Amelia Earhart lives on. People remember her accomplishments, her courage, her personal example of a woman's greatness.

Years earlier, before another flight, Amelia had written G.P.: "Please know that I am quite aware of the hazards. I want to do it because I want to do it. Women must try to do things as men have tried. When they fail, their failure must be but a challenge to others."

When I was in high school, one of my boyfriends took me for my first plane ride. We did spins and loops. Like birds, we soared in the air. I knew what Amelia meant when she said she flew for "the fun of it." As I wrote this book, I wanted you to feel the thrill of flying while you sat safely on the ground.

The week before I finished the last chapter, my father-in-law sent me an article from the *Abilene* (Texas) *Reporter-News* about Amelia Earhart. In September 1989, 52 years after she disappeared, a group of people searched the islands surrounding Howland, hoping to find Amelia's plane. They didn't find anything.

More than likely, the mystery will never be solved. Even so, the mystery of her death is not as important as her life. As a little girl, Amelia loved to read adventure stories. Boys were the heroes. Just once, she wished for an adventure story about a girl. Amelia Earhart wrote that adventure story with her own life.

—M.K.